SET HERE LIL RIOT

SET SLIGHT AGAIN THE DIRT

& FREE MY HAND

AHSAHTA PRESS
THE NEW SERIES

#87

QUARTET

C. VIOLET EATON

Ahsahta Press, Boise State University, Boise, Idaho 83725-1580
Cover design by Quemadura
Book design by Janet Holmes
ahsahtapress.org

LIBRARY OF CONGRESS CATALOGING-IN-PUBLICATION DATA

Names: Eaton, C. Violet, 1982– author.
Title: Quartet / by C. Violet Eaton.
Description: Boise, Idaho : Ahsahta Press, 2018. | Includes bibliographical
    references and index.
Identifiers: LCCN 2017055771 | ISBN 9781934103838 (pbk. : alk. paper) | ISBN
    1934103837 (pbk. : alk. paper)
Classification: LCC PS3605.A865 A6 2018 | DDC 811/.6—DC23
LC record available at https://lccn.loc.gov/2017055771

I am particularly grateful to the editors of *Aufgabe, BafterC, Cannibal, Cloud Rodeo, Colorado Review, Columbia Poetry Review, No Infinite, RealPoetik,* and *Yalobusha Review* for previously publishing earlier forms and variations of these pieces.

A special appreciation for Theatre Organ Radio by the American Theatre Organ Society, which was often tuned to subliminal volumes in the background.

CONTENTS

FOR SARA

Hustlers of the world, there is one Mark you cannot beat: the Mark Inside.

WILLIAM S. BURROUGHS

No matter where you are you are alone
and in danger—well
to hell
with it.

LORINE NIEDECKER

POEMS

HOW ABOUT A LITTLE SOUL MUSIC

Three bagpipe will soon come. Selah.
River's little-to-no-fish now, river's
Slow, selah. Summer's two fat rac
-coons crawling up & over the back
Porch rail, dos mapaches, fat
As dogs, hissing for scraps then
Run off by the decaudated cat. Selah.
Three bagpipe. I turned on the light.
Don't kid yourself, kid, it's always
Something : last night was a dream
About a movie called *Mercy*. Tonight
It's all just far too long. Now the light's
Come on, the man's rooster's a mile off
& so into it he crows each time I'm up
To piss : he's better than us persons,
Who only wish we could bust the head
Of language, who only dream a new

Plan to carve the words in right. Amen.
The way we'd haunt the word *snake*
Would be quaint but for the serpent.

THAT UNHASPING WHICH

from the decks of the city
Seemed mere hillocks carpeted w/ sorrel
& I wanted to go there, fabric of earth's
Interval, sure it fastened. Hidden
Beneath arsenic & bismuth I'd have found
A scrim of peace there.
Somewhere else tho it's autumn still,
Some colophon of smoke rising up
The magnolia grove (the white one
Wood is cut from then the white itself is
Cut from it. Within. As in, the center
Of your hand : an image projected there,
Yoked like a revenant to the palm's tall
Dark house. Hand that depicts, that shines
Like culm hewed hard out the mountain, cast
Out quick from the mountain. The hand
Directs the motion : *come image hither,*

& *hover over the television* (somewhere
There is a television emptied out, the image
Not empty tho, not *not* somewhere.

ABRACADABRA

You look swung missy :
Clasping that host of
Common teasel &
Spanish needles, wake-
      robin, 'nlisten :
With that swing set look,
Hips all gee & haw,
Not to watch you move
      's unthinkable
Like taking a blind
Moon off a French cut.
O in my same weird
Blue clattering sight
Missy you swung hard.
That clutch of flowers
      bound in a ribbon
Left outside the door :

Shoes & stockings in
Your hand & little
Bare feet on the floor.

FOR JABBO SMITH

Cook the steak in mucho butter,
Dress it in key lime honey &
Banana ketchup. The whitest rum,
The greenest egg : when it's peeled,
One can pattern the shell flecks, &
That's language (an exterior delimit
-ing an interior, entire unsubtle Egg.
& the fishcrow : *ohmigod, ohmigod*,
Everybody's got a speaking place.
It begins in the mouth, shakes
Loose from there, Cladys,
Each your cast turns open'd
& swung like a balisong blade,
Inconsistent but mortal gorgeous
Risk, wrist-to-finger. Yours was
A means by which to pour out
Clear up to the brim : to dissipate,

Then reappear, if only shadow :
A book still with its rattle.
A record with some play.

Cast myself & my studies into
The shear line : that line (infinitely
Slim, what divides bible from plug.
& there found a near-unity, Janus
-faced, in the theoretical
Space between open & closed.
The powerful itch to cause a change
In a matter, moving from one state
To another, only a few small tools :
Comb, hook, rake & halfdiamond
(extensions of a finger really, a heart
What reckon'd the code inside
Each text. Not given but taken. & so
Then I knew faith. That the house
Would keep. The deadbolt remain.
& trust in the lover who shackles an-
other, just for the pleasurable game.

But these are only contracts :
The house you can penetrate.
The lover who leaves.

POOR ONION

Some suckers live lyrically
By looking *in* the body. Poor suckers,
Poor math, pure omen. Other folk
Look to the outside, clutch at huff rags &
Try just to get to be nothing : maybe
Score a job down at the chicken plant,
Pulling feathers, cutting throats, best case.
Maybe they pass by, maybe annealed,
Attenuate, welcomng the angularity of age,
Poor number. Hail the great conflicts :
Man vs. the Stankin Ass Pit Void, or
Frankenstein vs. The Wolf Man. We could
Find suckers, stake them, pit them against.
We could take bets. A crowd could form,
Thrash its paltry capital, then as quickly
Disperse. They fight hard but none panther.
Their own truth hold out just one flower.

Me, I'm more sensitive than most.
I have a bouquet. Not truth.
I have not a bouquet. I have a bucket.

DER VORHANG

Die Doppeltür öffnet sich
STRINDBERG

Hey hey darkmans. Hey murder.
O well hi there secret creeper.
You were cruel to me & so I left. But
Soon enough it was I found your double :
The hair & eyes, the mouth & voice & sex.
For a time we laughed at you, hid
Among the rigging, we. It wasn't very
Long before your double found my own :
Left her ghost light on & mothlike came
He to the apron floating. I saw them
Kissing, saw her hook him to the flies.
O curtain that separates, that has not
Matter, presence, state, being, nor spirit,
Yet drawn it took for me to find awares :
That they was you & me & maybe we
Was still the same, but fragment
-ed, but undead. O hey, we : us

Crawling out the coffin to perform.
Ooh wee. Like vampires. The vivid
Red light of fire.

NO SPRINGS

Watling Scale Co.

the *reclamans*

Pindar

R. Duncan

HAVE YOU GAINED OR LOST
WEIGHT?   in the *soul,* I say
(to be particular.
Seems it must be
Some weight there
Pulls you up & back
& in both directions.
Must be some : they say
The true soul is unbaptised,
Unimmersible :
A cork on a net on a sea.
The rattletrap affixed
To the pawned instrument.
It's nothing.
Only
The possibility of no thing so
Being there :

A Michigan bank
-roll on
A millionaire walk

O but you must try the wine, must
Feel please my crêpe edge, crimped
& finger this foulard of silk twill,
This fox stole, decrepit, that I keep
Beneath my skirtses (which I lift.
It don't bother me in my black hat,
Mouth flapping : I wanted to freak
Them anyway, point out the trick
World in all its muggy smear & arc.
Lay me in the violincase laughing :
Ha ha, tu ne dis pas tout, il y a *hoc*,
A *hic*, a hiccup, a body : there is
something there—prior—speaks up
Against it, rises not in it. Someday
Sure I'll burn what I owe like tracing
A line cross a throat. But someone's
Dark moaning moodly, a music

Of spiritual poverty :
A dollar cacophany, a caterwaul,
Here & there a yip.

TO PERFORM THE ACT OF WRITING AT A DISTANCE

Set the beacon at Bet Hakkerem,
Blow the trómbone out the Pythodd
On Clarissa. Or simply you could slur
Your word into a microphone, it'll
Get there, like church, eventual.
Next thing is, you're out of pocket,
Tongue slack like a jackleg preacher,
Voice banging around in the ether.
A word leave a mouth & trace a line,
Be mark'd or hended on one's other side,
Unhistoried, unseen & ferried
Away in its dark limousine, chauffer'd
By alterity, most intimate electric &
Driver of the long method . . .
Was born *there*, finds his way *here* :
Wherefore. The space between resolves,
Conducts the message, which is always

Abandon &, (rarely, an omen.
Speed you, yes, speed you,
Aby the many courses.

Went an ailing. Went an opening.
Went undesigning.
Enacted "Put-live-things-in-you"
(in case you really are that close.
O but just admit the will is fecund, tho
Animated & daubed with a set of bones :
      spectry composessor which
Empty the self in filling the jigger.
Are you moving it?   I am not moving it,
This pencil : but my page is marked,
My glass goes clean, ti ti, ti ti. What did
You there see? (doesn't matter :
Only what sees you can matter.
A poem sees. It sings. The last man
On earth singing the first
Song ever written. Doesn't matter.
You go (:

You'll be seen never & by no
Low ringers, least not until later.
A-wop-bop-a-loo-mop.

HE HADN'T FED THE CNAKE

You have parboiled a hank of venison,
You have chiseled a wicked Farfisa.
You practically shout the truth at the bucket.
Someone said a heart is like a cloister :
Holds what you pent up with
& who got you that way.
Man being what he is, purgatory's
Likely a cut-n-shoot, a hustler's club,
& those that's ready don't dick around.
What does not wolver. Let them
Bring their water :
Above & through the earth move all
Materials, the inscrutability of.
Pyrite, bauxite, & under & in the schist, aer.
"Are you in the throes, pal?
"Do you need the antidote?
"One last tug from the goblin?

Out there's the world :
The window, the vigilant real.
The first five fingers of the hand.

FALSE LAMKIN

15

How durst I go down
Into such good company
Expecting a dream but got
A suffering note instead.
This regiment of lines,
Thir ambulatory rows
Ordered just so : peste!
Get you your Betsy.
Fetch a silver basin &
Ketch with it the heart's
Water : fill with it what
Floweth out a heart (is
what they told me. Tho
I know it's but a window
The intruder crawl
Through, looking. There's
Blood in th kitchen

& blood in th hall,
Blood in th stanzas
Where th figures did fall.

GOODBYE BOOZE

Please you to know the devil's
Dead in a johnboat.
& in hir wee weird end some
Play buckpitch or pedro.
They ante with, say, the same love
One has for one's first dog or
For the wife of a friend
The instruments of will hold you
Back from. O sunny decimals
That scatter the changeable
Circumference of being : see that
If he buries something, turn it over.
Sing the old thing keeps you from
Reruns of damask, dried posies,
Pictures of Maria Callas all
Tacked to the clapboard :
The blind will to divine courage,

For what is courage but holding the hatchet :
The wind scalps the appletree.
The wire of song binds a mouth.

MIDSIZE COMBO THREE HORNPLAYERS
TIGHT BACKLINE

Little tuned up & way out in front. Not in it,
You'll not have had that, they'll say you're all tattered
Raiment, & no mystery. Lay that whammy any
-way : a loose vamp bodged with irregular horn stabs,
Straight pattern you can slink to, crowding
The air in the Tip-Top Lounge, contra legis
& rightly oughta, (be, : like magic, with your top hat
& white gloves you could extract the rabbit.
Move closer, it's almost over :
To wall off a bad path's as necessary as
Searching for a good one, & moreso. Count it.
This is how it happens :
You might tender temptation 'til jooked by love,
That's most, stuck on its shrike-stick &
Stood out in the yard show. You might
Shoot out the one light & darken the field to panick.
Or heel tap to a riff walk. Oye, dolor . . .

I told your ass before. When
I became unmanageable.
Motherfucker, I'm talking to you.

TO MY OLD ONES

It were like every mean-thought
Word led to another, & that I regret,
Truly, if regret is a hand to be dealt
In the final play. Most days
My library sends me up,
Same way I send a letter. Precisely
One paragraph in the literature
Where the idiot seems happy
(truly, & you read that one to me
Repeatedly. Most nights
Some book will take me outside
Past the thicket, down the stairs
& into hell . . .   it's nothing, it's
Boredom (that's what hell is :
One gets older, one hopes
It gets less tender, the number
Of drums or drugs that enter.

One hopes the second ½ pint don't hit
½ as hard as your first, Lord knows
I have a voice, but it's not the one I use.

PRIVATION

I had 460 lbs. of pure hell, Gramps had
That deep good clear radio voice
Racked tho by Kools, he said *son, do you*
Think you know what love is? No sir I did
Not think. *Let you look at this gimmick*
& spread his fingers out clawlike, pointing
Downward, & he flashed once real bright,
A strip of molybdenum, hot & chartreuse
Like that & then gone. So I just waited,
Pained & not mended. Grappled with con
-sequence, there involute. Like the song, it'd
Have to do. Until the real thing comes along.
Until then it's high & misty. O grant me
No love, Lord it hurts like heat. It may
Take the astringent, the witch hazel to rid it.
May take more than a decade's time,
& Hanna riding me, wiping my brow,

Shhhhhhhhhhhh she's saying,
There there now she's saying,
There there inchoate earthen speck.

HIC EST DOCTUS

Here's what I want to have said, as I were
Waving this wand & lit from under :
The 'I' that performed once out in the open
He had confidence in his intellectual casuistry
& came into his stanzas with peerage
Until what he thought dawn which broke on him
Whereupon he made a condition of voice herself
& sent his other hand about dallying
In the mellow air of habitation.
I have of late, but wherefore I know not, assumed
Within the skull queer shadows   :
Some geometry, some rhetoric.
I found the vague shape the head forms
The skull exhibits also
Except the eyes are larger & it laughs.
Skull that porters a broth of stars which will
Imbricate & be laid at your feet like a wreath.

Which is all that I can offer you.
I still have that thing you offered me
Which of course I never took.

US & THE BAD MEN IN THE ELM PLACE

Snort of rookus, poison'd
Spike on rear ricasso, & they're
Good to empt a man.
Don't it feel peccant, how many
Windows they broke?   the way
They rubbed their jaws like that?
It's enough to raise allovers
& the damnd vellications, o
It's a Lon Chaney Christmas :
Sun pale yaller & hung
Like a cape, halfassed in its last
Look at the world.
Us & the bad men, godblessit.
In the elm place. Each of them
Esau : one woman on either side,
One dexter & one sinister.
But not a single one was witness

To our honings. If you forget
Them they are gone. We're
All gone. Our real movement.

COME SOME HUNGER

Come to the house some time :
I'll wear my finest Sunday blood cloak
Right out of the prior midnight
Soul lying open (that's just a joke
So laugh, you drag . . .
My own cussedness like
Smoke leaks out from under the porch eave
Glitters like diamonds & cracks like a gunshot.
I'm standing nose to bottle
Heartfelt, & had intention
Redeemed I would have gentle prodded
Won't you have a drink with me?
Don't, & it'll sting me some . . .
It's a boy down there
That shadow around the parlor.
It's a man down there
Unearths the heavy stain :

Come body, arise
Violet. Little hysterical pilgrim.
Little pillar.

FRAGMENTS

low-slung the sky lurks

mauve in its transition

brooks a lonesome company slack of stars

Listen,

I'm pulled to do wrong | It's my dull talk
I got the authority | Check my architecture

---

often I am   :   am I visited

haunted inured
in what space

personally I have
told some clear things
some Names for

Set here lil riot
Set slight again the dirt
& free my hand

---

each day containing sevral cymbals
that rattle 'round the host of it
each day containing sevral horses
each day containing equal horses

---

that abandon
stave off that abandon
I believe is what made calamity
course through
the os of your heart
    you abettor you
Student

<u>books quoted</u>   (first edition

Glassine wrapper not present

           but the window it was throws shapes :

& out of it come summer
afflicted, different

     some years
you to you heard it not

& yet :   people trick themselves

in each breast
a west   an east

Old roan pony stay away
the sycamores unnatural

---

been off juice since three towns back of
cedar pinning a glade

& now tentatively stand & tremble easily-
known in night's shawl

it's like a slow burn
moon in the wires

\\

(but I spent that piece

HOW FROM HORSE
into horse poem
it goes :

lowly
& slowly

<u>Whole heap a little horses</u>

& such pittance poems —

Torn dress, page-brown
As if a familiar air
Lit up made the room
Made hesitant somehow

    ashen & fragrant
& Thats like mine breast

Earl Bostic, Earl Hooker, Earl Palmer, Earl King

Earl Wild. Earl Scruggs. Earl Fatha Hines

"Duke of Earl," Gene Chandler

PREACHER :

     or rather, the
viper in his god habit
     Let him know
that where he levies
     I'll collect

---

wouldachokeme
(that one word
and I'm – look – I'm
rusty but no
not too low
Damn sure still
I have
these fast hands

---

some words ~~are~~ blunted
some came into focus

some arranged to meet my blue noise of

others jitter, blather

a few bend low & flatter

---

white pine like a wave
(both object & motion
within it resonance

---

   time to bless
the fucken
sea snakes again

LITTLE FLOWER

in a field of rye where the question
which is most beautiful
is obsolete

hewn in its own myth but
cured in the fact of thinking &
crushed into a whole

<u>books quoted</u>   (dictionary

supplement   corrigenda   list of spurious words

Yon chickens snicking   like sad rattles

<u>I'm in my cups</u>

I'm born in the caul

imbued w/ the virtue of fascination

   "it's not right
to cut a man off so quick
right in midair . . .

---

hell you still can swing 1 quarterpint
Red Spot chaser on county papers,

drink the spirits of lit loggerhead shrikes
& show the rope some flowers Why Not

a deertick lands &
it's on a hopeful bridge
somewhere
my Tenant who augur belief

<u>Borage in Fever</u> | an inversion of thirds :

like touching you produced the most feral clucking

white tshirt like a lens announcing the inner

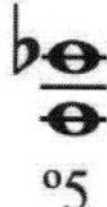

anyways it's
all dead pegged

the card come up cold label

it's night again
open at the blouse

there : it closes now
& we are quits
the clouds
acomplish a symmettrie

like dun tits wrapped in tulle

    vedic colors
crown the perimeter

& weensy starses tap their claims

Anything depleted
(rose lilac potato
Where a description lies still
bleating even words in iamb

I remember every variation   :
                every declamation, laden

laden with what?   w/ triumph,   w/ heckle

low oh woe own some

<u>books quoted</u>   (exemplary volume

swept & garnished
Edges (deckled — rough enough to make clear
poetic meditation on its subject
w/ attendant drawings
type design 16th c. Fr.   (by Granjon
ct, st ligatures
Lilac script initials on rag paper
& illus. by Smithsonian process

----

what objects was & pure
or the order they have
have they order

What frequent deceive

Whear am I limb

Heart of bat w/ red silken string

3 cuttings rue bark by the axe

---

vans cities rents miles hands

---

drunk is big in its
feelings   folks

stoned is maximal
tho
stuck on a detail

THE
BODY
IS
A
NARROWS

straight & sharp

is a line that
at least once
limns up
from negation

---

who do you believe?

    ~~you're~~ your endearingly small

habit descending

    white & difficult structure

we're the last people to leave town
what we do is hidden there
we live & work amongst

People can be pretty
    bad magpies
Flush from their ever having
Any effort at all When
Even a pretty coin
Would not tempt . . .

KEEP HOLD
YOUR WALLET
&
YOUR CHRIST
—MOMS

---

every is fever
to meaning

elsewhere is
a used one, most
unsettling

---

who're
the hitters   the haters
the haters' haters

what false hades
came first out the low ditch?

la ha from the charm of
it

sure
seems evry hollow is
benighted by secrets

(cattle gate at Lake Sequoyah

(bad sign of water moving upward

~~jim stark~~
~~jett rink~~
~~cal trask~~

UNITED PENTE
-COSTAL

All
man has some
bottle Always
with his Satan

<u>about a inch from the wood</u>

the saw gets hungry
ONCE HE SEEN

Ben don't work much anymore
        speaking but his
    well allowed remarks
                lord he got paid tho
            $ rising up beyond the margin . . .

        That his old antic particle still
    stirs in the vertebrae
                can't be but admired

<u>rich is the day salt</u>

day can thunk bucket

roots diminish & brown

            Bayou Geneve

THERIAULT :   "Oil fire out there some ways"

        (keys wallet on the small table
                glass of water very much quit

Where's Nino?

"He's on the mayonnaise again
          "He
just couldn't cut
the mustard

---

                              pig in | hen out

<u>these our records of sense</u>

dogs in the road
          (a very few
as if just one
had sundered

                    : :

fire
clearing out
a room

<u>prison art</u> on a en
     -velope, handlettered
& handdrawn : crude shell of

disney's Bambi alongside
a bluebird, narco lyrics, a knife

<u>what I did before poetry bored</u>

mostly hung tight trying
to dial it in

<u>. . . contd.</u>

I went around those days, went
around *in* them,
   in the winter of them.

'til the juniper come out half-sunk
& spring cours'd the bees.

I woke & got dressed
   this one restaurant where I go   & pretty
the way the drive there is feeling of phenomena,

PLACE THE RADIO UPON THE STAIR
THE RADIO MOVES IT FLOATS UP

Look up into the air
Space where the sound expired
& noticing calm now throughout the plot
Set up the jug plonk | plastic cup

PICTURE

broom lying there but. That
pitcher ain't broke.

---

pork bones 1.39/lb. today
eggs 2 dollars   dried noodles 3 for 5
1 quart 5w-30 motor oil $4.22

claw hammer, 20 oz. (wood handle
sixteen dollars twenty four cents

---

ah wife! :
melodies frame your husband's

vagabond brain
to a thin weak fretting!

---

the small creek
run out
the mouth of the cave

where water
meets
its meager allotment

meager water
  but that it travels
& enjoins

---

young young river
his greater Power to deliver

his Other power

made by a dragging

<u>man,</u>

was not touch made by child

its aft xmas
so

buck
the cut tree

ruck it
down,   hoo

<u>unbutton this magic shaker</u>

one not ever shook the ground when it has walked
one not ever even shook the gourd

<u>thrown th rag up high</u>

no dumb moves, tho | it's | not America's cloth

---

the bog at the north end of the grocery lot
we frequent :
     someone pushed a cart down the long slope
& now it half-rides the ditchwater
the same way the sun do,   *parched.*

~~bellow cluck grunt~~
there is this lone carrion brain   that's

Rain turns me over
a quickening per se
that I attain a degree of gumption
beside the pale moon

---

out hung / hung out

house been Quaking
ma was various
Both real open
when you have to be home

I'm the gravedigger
I'm the undertaker
            I'm the dead man
            I'm the preacher

<u>you be 1890 dollface</u>

A man weren't meant to fly
A man weren't meant to fly

---

whiskey = a pessary
halfburied in millet

rye = handsaw to the egg

gin is where I stood long,
Died with my collar out

±

au revoir pls write
p.o. box 234
inveil the back of the envelope

refract the tender missal
retract the former title
every recto has its verso
each flower & his thistle

<u>Rural harmonics</u>

aye, breathsome spruce
the veery alights
upon
then fox sparrow

pine tree does something

Ⅲ

what are symbols?

a skull : sometime shown with two crosst bones : an hourglass w/ wings
   anchor : bat : broken column : drooping candle : bee
a hooded robe : upended torch : the broken tools of trade

---

are there others?

skeleton worm serpent scythe : evergreens & ivy
   the cypress tree : the fir : the bay : lilies palm & wheat
a weeping willow : rosemary :
                              violet   :   myrtle   :   yew

On the part of her
Portrait most distant
Sure
        upon her mind
& unopened eyes

This morning
        standing
Silver against

---

singing together

sheer joy of singing

H O N O R eat you from the inside, like a hagfish.

•

C O N S C I E N C E is for some a rope to hang.

•

B L A M E the rope its knot.

•

P O V E R T Y inquires as I account the day.

Desires death there; a numinal pleasure.

•

However P L E A S U R E ' s windows to the good soul.

•

Poets are exempt from death though when our eyes close he is
present always.

•

P R E S E N C E nearly always marked in eyes.

The hand commands what touching does but sound what starve the lips.

•

L U C K is a loss held in abeyance : L U C K is loss accruing interest.

B A D L U C K its own interest : *to have built a fortune from misfortune.*

•

The one thing about T H E I N E F F A B L E is that it's not fucking effable.

•

Odhran.

•

It is true that the library occasions the haunting of the house.

•

F R E E D O M is not the problem, but its taxonomy.

•

& that the Artist give every man his state.

FICTIONS

THE CAPE TRICK

When Baby Dodds met Moondog. Gamera met Gojira. Mickey Chicken
met The Stinger. The theater was unlocked & empty so I entered.

The mysterious feat of walking. The seats with their black velvet. Termi-
nal wiring. The smoke pocket, the wings. The wrack & ruin.

Me, I didn't have 5¢ in my early teens falling from the earth.
But I thought forward & had precognition.
I thought one condition of late-alcoholic movements performed under
the one light pinning the interior of the theater was the emptying of
certain jurisdictions the self imposed.

Let me say first :

        at birth I made no distinction between bilious & phleg-
matic, bituminous & anthracitic. Between snakes or ladders, beetles or
stones.

Papa put 'WOLF KILLED SERVICE' up at the station, & picking &
shaking we cogitated directly (I was three
I had carried outright the funeral rigging a long distance. Well so what,
that's what it was. & it was during that same system it appeared in
sevral ads under sevral names.

You know, those typical hexwerke pamphlets (they were all fixed,
having the exception that everywhere those same agents performed rites
such as bathing, rapture, expert cunnilingus.
"wash here"   (they might have said   "come redefine yourself"   "sell
veneer & talcum to the willing client . . .

Age 11 I wrote "Georgia Horn" sometimes on the back of the bus seat,
not sure what it meant.

I wrote PRACTICE FOLK SEX | PRACTICE EVERYWHERE

That's okay, I was taught to grip the evidence til it breaks & I did (this
was now seventh grade (I had caught pox had become a loathsome ap-
pearance. I had this faded full uncle, a ½ lunger hung up on 16mm w/
sync sound. He'd take me to the theater & I'd cut those shapes

Yes, a fine unbridled time. & so I was bricoleur. & so it was that I created
my first art.

For my next art, a smallish quoin that bosomed up. Then a double-LP
with enlarged centerhole, sun warp & tip-on gatefold. The first two
sides were cast cool, but side three ran an ashen curse.   The
last I can't speak of.

Absorbed these records through the mouth. Wept.

Finally at nineteen I acquired literacy, wondered WAS MARIE DE
FRANCE A WITCH   (I wanted to know & the library indicated it
She had magic the public could not tend : in Jesusname they jinxed her
into "theology."
The mean distribution of Methodist practicum had some high hard de-
gree of magick but was alas besot in kraut brine.

        I read *York's Psalms for Women* (you wouldn't know it — it was
printed privately
        & I consumed the only copy. It had valuable admixtures but it
was a time I was trying to flee knowledge . . .

When I returned to the theater after a long absence something inside me
had changed or maybe it was the theater itself, something altered. Some-
body's mysterious prints defiling the room a little.
But that same damn uncle, hanging on. Had to show me some :

Onscreen, it was 1964. & he moved. The man.
Like a river my love took me in & cut into money.
I lost my head about it.

Over & over & again.

The Pentecost says *slain in the spirit*.

(& when you saw the film you realized fully half
of it was darkness. Unperceived. If one could slow it down, a series of
timed signals — light, like a metronome, then its absence. Holding the
room still.

I am immune now at 34. Now that I know death by residual technology.
Now that I know S T O P when red. That I know meadowlark & I know
certain sweet airs come forth & call home blossoms. I know animals. I
have been to their locations. I know their deep winter. I know water,
mountains, threshed grasses. I know acres.

But still I remember when I was a wild kid, like when I was 19 when I
could go off a couple times & still come out hard. I got money in that
bottle & I'm not leaving yet. Even now, when I got some young thing in
the high waist green short crawling around on the leopard spread with
the Specialty sleeve & a cracked 45 rave-up b/w goatskin drums.
Even now I got things to do. I got my own dreams.
I think about how I'd go up against a Stratotone & hang a dominant-7 on
it. I think about the top 13 witch flicks, the top ten horror films that ar-
en't just shapes of fear, the 20 underground movies not worth bleeding
for. I advocate glamor every day, I think.

I think about the man in that film. How he'd shown me how to move,
shown me moving. How a little, like how that's like. A little to the side.
A little. A little. A little leg out. A little leg shaken. A howl. A little to
the sides. How to fall. To the knees. & rise. A little more. When it's a hip
us wants. It's like a little death. See it shimmy like that. Now it's a show.

SIX SCENES IN SEQUENCE

I. THE BEGINNING

See the man in the suit. The man in the morning. In the evening.
The man in the suit.
Driving his car. Taking his time.

2. THE WAITING

The looking. The watching.

3. THE KILLING

Lit cigarette on its end in the corner, that's incense.
While he do.

4. THE DETAIL

The other man. The unfortunate.
The man with the number tattooed on his neck.

5 . THE MISTAKE

He didn't use the pay phone. Not all of them are gone yet—
Look outside the taquería, the laundromat. A few clinging on.

6 . THE ESCAPE

The man imprisoned.
Cutting parts off. Mailing them outside his cell.
Each envelope, another part of himself.

Hey now, it's bright out.

& SO DO WE CARRY IT ALONE

August was deathly, the hours overadequate, and I just withered to the page. Had little responsibility other than each morning's coffee; perhaps to notice with some interest, say, the drapes vaguely admitting a certain vacuous light. All sorts of minor individuation.
There was a small shape in the middle of the window screen on the west side of my room. I imagined a previous owner was applying sealant around each windowpane & the tar got in the wire mesh & hardened there.

It looked just exactly like a tiny Japan.

Sometimes in the late afternoon when the sun came in at a low angle, I stopped whatever it was I'd been working on, stretched in my chair, & looked at the shape. I imagined I could go into it if I wanted, go into the little Japan & stay there a while.

O but that isn't the lens. This owns.

Directly behind the house the growth crept in & choked out the boundary lines. Red trumpet honeysuckle, contemptible wretch. Curséd, bulbéd vine :   Let me ride it out alone.
I detested fecundity, longed for a desert or an arid plain. Some evenings were spent staring at the advancing curtain in back. One found me trying to cut through, but I was just one dull blade & never I'd get those hours again.

The turk's cap cactus I still kept under glass, to remind me of another
place, small glass icosahedron, with brass bevels.

. . .

Not that any of it helped. *Verb one art in the hand*, they said, *it won't
matter.*
Hallelujah, roll away . . .

My face was just this sunken lane, an enervating dissolution that had
the appearance of continuity. My discourse therefore suffered. Pubic hair
itched.

Hounded, I hid within the social. Trawled both sidewalk and bar, seek-
ing refuge amid the so-called poets.
But would you believe at first they decided it was unsuitable for me to
make an appearance? That my fine clothing mocked their sensibilities?
I had to reflect & adapt. Else I were to be excluded from their canon.
O for shame.

It took a spell to adopt that kind of display. It cost.
I even did a murder once.
Hell, I *solved* a murder once.

He, I mean I (I mean he— I tried these many things that soon became
a rumor. Some have even been in my head & found one other person is
there. It's so much better that way, don't you think? My sweet lost lamb
. . . How ever will he get back home to friends?

. . .

The rain fell in the bar bathroom, continued to fall. It seldom rained
there except in winter when the water'd move slowly over the mirror.
But that precisely : for it was sudden winter.

A widening vacuity which I entered, hesitant.

To open the door & start the motor.

That one boy there in the bar kept saying your name wrong & so I
smacked him. He didn't *know*. Or rather *remember* . . .
But I suppose memory's a trick curated from a distance. Believe it passes
through everybody. Difference is I write it down.
What I believe.
They pass through everything & I write them down.

. . .

It had been years that we had seen one another, then an evening sleep
bristled with your form.
When at last I awoke in my humid chair, I proposed refretting all the
instruments according to the Archytan system :

This would allow me to express the enharmonic genus of the classical
Phrygian scale.

        But I'm not always going out of my life. Or to act it. I
lived for a while ago & the fact was not always immediately clear. Why
do we have to be able? What do we even have? Sure you can be the

white paper, I'm so damn blank.
& just for the first time since the beginning of the day (& so much for
the rest of it.

Drawn up again in my manse. The inside was still dim, draped in the
bruise. The little shape in the screen . . .

& the car out back, her windshield's cracked & spidered
                                    which reminds me : the drive-
way's been sealed, but come autumn it will gator (Albert Pinkham Ryder

INDETERMINACY (OR, CONVERSELY THE PATTERN

Myth is the facts of the mind made manifest in a fiction of matter.

MAYA DEREN

Along the path, the arm, descends, with flower, from above, the hand,
places the flower, the flower, is, carried, by, a woman, the woman,
ascending, the stairs, the door, locked, the key, produced, the purse,
closed, the key dropped, the key retrieved, the door unlocked, the door,
opened, the woman, passing, through, the door.

The interior scene, &, the table set, a cup, of coffee, a heel, of bread, a
knife, falling, from, the bread, the phone, off, its hook, the woman, as-
cending the stairs, the curtain, moving, like a flag, the record, in its case,
the record, playing, the record, slowing, the arm, removed, the woman,
descends, the stairs, the patterned chair, where, the woman sits, the
hand, places the, flower, the hand, strokes, the breast, the eye, closes,
slowly.

. . .

Along, the path, as if, through a tunnel, the eye, recedes, the hooded
figure walks, along, the path, the figure, turns, the face, a mirror, the
woman, stops, the figure, walks, &, the woman, runs, the figure, with
the flower, around the corner, the woman, runs, the woman, slows,
ascends the stairs, the woman's face, the door, opened, woman passing,
through the door.

The interior scene, the knife, the woman, ascends the stairs, curtain,
moving, like, a wave, the woman's face, the phone, unhooked, on, the

bed, the sheet pulled back, the knife, a kind, of, mirror, the woman's
face, the phone, hung up, curtain moving, like a shroud, the woman
falls, the space, compressed, the stairs, unhinge, become, an arch, wom-
an, passing, through the arch.

. . .

The interior scene, as if, above, the patterned, chair, the woman, sitting,
a record, plays, the record, in its case, the arm, removed, woman sleep-
ing, a woman, watching, the window, out, the window, along, the path,
a figure, walks, the figure holds, a, flower, woman, running, woman,
looking, around the corner, a woman, stops, ascends, a stair, a key,
produced, a mouth, closed, a hand, a key, a woman passing, through, a
door.

An interior, scene, a figure, ascending, a stair, a figure, holds a flower,
passing through, an, arch.

. . .

Space, motion, stairs unhinge, the figure, place, the, flower, on, the bed,
woman calling, figure turning, face, a mirror, woman calling, figure,
vanished, woman, motion, displace, disrupt, woman, looking, a knife,
a chair, a pattern, woman sleeping, a figure walking, along, a path,
around, a corner, a woman, runs, slows, a woman turns, ascends, a stair,
a key, produced, a hand, a knife, passing, through a door.

The table set, the women sitting, woman watching, walking, carries a
knife, knife against, breast, hand, place, the knife, become, the key, the
woman sits, the key, retrieved, the key, produced, the hand, the key,
again, the black hand, the knife, the plan, is hatched, the plot, to kill,
displace, disrupt.

                            .   .   .

Along the beach, the woman, slow, the knife, come, slow, eyes, open,
slow, a man, a flower, he, hangs the phone, ascends the stair,
     the, woman slows, the, table set, pass arch,

          ascend stair,

     the man, the flower, the bed, the mirror, the man's face, the mirror
retrieved, the woman, the flower, the hand, strokes, the breast, the lips,
the man, the music, the, flower, vanish, the, eye, the, knife, the, man,
the, face, the mirror broke.

                            .   .   .

Along the beach, the shards, of glass, the water, & its wave, moving,
like, a curtain, moving, again.

Along the path, the man, he, walks, ascends, retrieves, unlocks,   he
passes.

The interior scene, the, pattern, shards,
                              the chair,   the glass,   ~~THE END~~.

THE INTERVAL

I think it was summer. Yeah : Nicolas was in the wheatfield. I remember because I was near him, though I felt at the time captive. Fettered in summer's arcade between the hot air where it puckered. I couldn't reach him, Nicolas. His arms were out : I'm sure it was summer.

Ollie had blood on his second knuckle. The ball lay where he had hit.

.   .   .

Before mine supper the sky descends, most certain. Every night.

& every day I carried off to school. The back of the schoolyard met the bridge that rose out over the highway.
Some years spun out from that, slow. There would be another school. & another : a Greek revival : Doric columns & a dry lawn. The first check. First gasoline. I made seed in the girl, in the bed.

Under the pin oak it rained always.

If I closed my eyes then, the pleasant rushing. Like trucks near the on-ramp.

Then prom.

Learned two trades. Lost part of a finger. Sent for daisies, 2 x 2s & screws, some vinegar. Sent for my one horse. All this from my book of facts.

. . .

We stole what would not be missed. Me, Ollie, Nicolas. Me & my one
horse. Yeah : it might have been summer. Was a movie played near town
a ways, off South Furnace, I don't remember the name. You could ask.

THE WHITE HOUSE BY THE BLACK RIVER

On or about September 29, the lawyer did knowingly mail the snake, a live one, venomous, *Agkistrodon contortrix*.

Someone called the sheriff.

Someone called the pathologist.

It wound up dead in ethanol, in a jar for the jury to see.

The lawyer he pled guilty, & the judge he took it easy : a believer in redemption, he felt the man had "seen the light."

. . .

In the white house by the Black River, Perkins used to torch it in the bulb.

He played mancala.

He drew the compound bow.

Six miles south-southeast, Cloady ran the pits in the river. One of them grabbed a branch in its mouth, big as a whale jawbone. Think on Samson who slew a thousand. Think on old Jonah.

. . .

Later they found funnels, pumps & residues. Pharmaceuticals & copper line. Some plastic two-liters, cut & reassembled.

They found the corpses of fifty-seven dogs.

Fifty-seven dogs fed sleeping pills hid in frankfurters. Shot between the eyes.

They found the evil men do.

.   .   .

This rail skinny tweak, he was already out of there, he called himself *Le cuisinier,* "the cook." & really was once, they said, little short-order grease joint, burnt up they said, not even a foundation they said. Liars. Devils. Culprits. Can't even ask a body for the true word, everybody worked here then is gone.

The cook indeed. Though his techniques were altogether more refined—

SMOKED EEL, FENNEL BULB
9,10-didehydro-N-(2-hydroxy-1-methylethyl)-6-methylergoline-8-carboxamide

CURRANTS, OX HEART, BLACK BUTTER, ASPIC
(+)-10,11-dihydro-5-methyl-5H-dibenzo [α,δ]cycloheptene-5,10-imine

PIGSFOOT, STEWED CARROTS
dextroamphetamine sulfate

5-(2-chlorophenyl)-1,3-dihydro-7-nitro2H-1,4-benzodiazepin-2-one,)

.   .   .

In the pineywoods by the penitentiary, the recluse whittled & sketched.
At or about midmorning. He drew figures of indeterminate sex. Thought
back on his testimony. Remembered his first wife.

It had been then a grim & jagged night, the newbie flew around town
kiting checks. Hanging big paper. Two men hauling a large tire in the
back ways that aren't on maps. Same two hauled out of the lake some
few days later. The wife had cut the story from the front page news.

.   .   .

"That hit me hard, man. Ain't gonna never get over this. I can't.
I can't, they took a big part of me, (says it from behind the respirator

Then what you run for ?   "ohhhhh, well . . . strictly for sensation.

It's not a difficult question—

Q : *Are you rebellious?*
A : Yes, but almost quietly
      & alone
      like a car abandoned in the woods or a severed finger left in a
      kraft bag.

How do you structure your answer. By accident. Almost like a key detail
the police let slip. *A police*, that's the singular, what they prefer. Most of
us don't at all. Prefer them. Trespassers. Malefactors. Pigs. Active in the
klavern. Tear it all up & let's start over.

.   .   .

On or about December 13. The night spent as a two-bit medium at the
Whitehall Motel, just trying to recoup a little of the needs of the dead.
You take a pill to fall asleep. & soon it's
El Dorado Jane Doe dragging something through the sky :

        a strip of cloth, a thin scratching in black ink
If you could suss it, it's her real name & not the one she gave out (same
as a foreign luxury car make.
Instead it's another night you're soaked in sweat, sat up quick & fighting
to suck in a real breath . . .

.   .   .

HOGTAILS & RAMPS
1-chloro-2,2,2-trifluoroethyl difluoromethyl ether

PONE OF HOECAKE, BLACK PAINT
α-amino-2,3-dihydro-3-oxo-5-isoxazoleacetic acid

50-ODD RICH PEACHES IN BLOOD W/ CUMIN
xxxxxxxxxxxxxxxxxxxxxxxxxxxxxxxxxxxxxxxxxxxxxxxxxx

.   .   .

There was a place . . . well that's not exactly right. The right word. Say it anyway. Place between the hills where the station didn't reach, the conjunto one. A static occasionally breached by inaudible Spanish.

You were able to pull in another though, just skittering across the rice fields as if through water, touched by a faint coppery tang where it rubbed against the sides of silos :

there's a jukebox playin | just a half a block down | saying I'm goin to the river | gonna jump right in & drown

but i ain't gonna do that, girl | no, no | I'll just keep on hangin around

.   .   .

There was a place. Not a location but a zone.

.   .   .

Some moved from ripping to cooking to interstate smuggling. They found the evil men do.

Men who'd lay bets on anything : cockfights, trick shots, dominoes, craps. Other men's lives. Their mahjongg games with the Filipino rules.

The unclaimed were laid to the potter's field while the missing remain in some ditch.

.   .   .

DRIED BEEF, GRISTLE, PARSNIPS & POTATOES
dextromethorphan hydrobromide

SALT, SOUSE, CIGAR
(+)-107-chloro-1-methyl-5-phenyl-2H-1,4-benzodiazepin-2-one

BONE, SALAD, MILK
α-pyrrolidinopentiophenone

.   .   .

That martini glass tat. That shape.
Curtis had a friend put it on him when he was nineteen & raising hell. A
stick-n-poke, all it took was a sewing needle & some ink from a felt-tip
pen. Back of the left hand, just a small outline in the fleshy web between
forefinger & thumb.

There was a photograph once, the two of them
standing just outside the wig store. & that was then, & that's enough,
but sometimes . . .

.   .   .

On the state road near the county line.

There was a place there, on that road, in the night hours.
        A few men walked
or rather, were drawn forward
            as if the line were a lodestone (which it were, of sorts :
            just over was the closest bonded liquor.

79

A few men walked
or rather, loped unevenly with hunched necks. These material dead,
proceeding to the horizon, consumed from the inside out.

Most walked with backs to traffic. Bad idea :
some Rockefeller making for that same line   . . . & just like that.

.   .   .

GOOSE EGG, FRIED BREAD, RED SALT, RAISINS
3,4-dimethyl-2,5-dimethoxyamphetamine

LARD
toluene

<u>Postlude</u>

Someone shot up Perkins. They found him on his bed, feet flat on the
floor. Like he tried to stand up.

They found the dogs.

They exposed the ring.

.   .   .

It's been rain all week (think on Noah.

Last night a low spot in the levee crested : sixty acres of wheat under,
sixty hay too.

But that was a good long way from here,

150 miles away last night in Toad Suck, Arkansas.

THE CABARET

Mi mama no quiere, mi papá tampoco, que yo vaya al cabaré

SEXTETO BOLOÑA

the lack of separation of
the blank from the real
the image from the actual
the erotical from the political
the venereal entertainment from
the artful performance
the louche display wherein
the acts come one atop
the other, first
the barbershop quartet then
the can-can dancers then
the comedian then
the contortionist then
the ventriloquist then
the ape man then
the hermaphrodite then
the drugged bear on the bicycle then
the mentalist then
the wrestlers then
the drag show then
the blow-off then
the two men spinning plates then
the fire-eaters then
the hustle happened easy then
the steer chose the mark
the shade blocked his vision &
the stick kept him close
the wire skimmed the pocket
the duke removed the take

the car crossed the center

the fist broke the glass

the geek bit the chicken

the letter reached the post

the branches snaked open

the songbirds sailed out

the crepuscular animals admitted

the road forked where it couldn't

the dirt road cut back of

the main stage

the midway

the midden

the sign upon the midden say beware

the hornet spooklight, beware

the white lady

the strange passenger

the apparitional car

the phantom handprint on the window

the crying child under the bridge

the vanishing hitchhiker

the vardøger

the shadow government

the leaky roof circuit

the air monkey

the bad order

the calliope

the collapse

the young ones that understood it all

the private masque

the $$ stacks

the miser w/ his dice in jail
the little correction of values on the edge of debt
the being-toward brave death
the air a strong founding
the cause of downright sentiment
the path by which they come to occupy
the nearer sense
the leaf's tax
the supreme branch
the supreme vision
the true vine
the root
the mouth of whole gold teeth
the glass atop the piano
the jaguar statuette
the hat in the hand
the fleet of long black cars idling outside
the gorgeous women
the fire which invites fools
the mystery of business
the beginnings of circles
the influence of lines
the congress in the big room
the liquor shared amongst
the liquor kept wholly to oneself
the ass-back of culture
the one that we get down to
the liar in the gibbet
the onion in the stew
the wild little art flick

the sacramental wound
the joke caught laughing w/
the one that wasn't
the illness that began low
the hot skin that kept
the away blood kept
the breath w/in
the breath cold
the breath spinning
the bowl ringing
the petal yielding to pale hue
the red dress back in its ambry
the small cut of her mouth
the basilectal whir of her mouth
the mouth which is connected w/
the disposable & w/ fear anxiety delivrance
the mouth moving from law to lawlessness
the preteen leaning out the window to smoke
the dropped coin in the box
the keyed number
the snakehips & the arms up
the tank top the gold jewelry &
the palm tattoo & then
the record ending
the talk ceasing
the armadillos jumping
the river jumping
the harmonium winging
the roses subsect
the whiskey burns

the image winnows
the stars influence the three nations
the earth the sky & water
the dobsonfly the hellgrammite dwell in all three
the stiletto kicks in the hand
the money spawns on the table
the diamonds shine on the rail
the mob sweating the action
the player dogging the nine
the stock still room
the little truth
the amphetamine grip
the show reveals its purpose, it's
the apparitions of john, opening w/
the ruy lopez, then
the morphy defense, then
the norwegian variation, then
the deathy film lain to the earth
the automata of al-jazari
the wandering handkerchief
the disappearing grain
the cut-and-restored ribbon
the mysterious self-filling lota
the thayer's super-vanish of doves
the breather crimp
the riffle force
the hindu shuffle
the hofzinser bottom
the hambone
the hamadryad

the con job
the anteluca
the foundry
the clerk
the cakewalk
the catwalk
the catafalque
the coracle
the tipi
the tenebrist
the hat brim
the hat trick
the trick bag
the bag lunch
the miserere, swung
the ballpark organist
the last castrato
the bad rung of the last ladder
the pysanka
the raisin wine
the plum wine
the dandelion wine
the corn beer
the fishcake
the popskull
the white mule
the red horse
the colt
the cribbing colt
the mare

the cymbal
the cigarillo
the sangre de paloma
the junco
the misfit
the poet
the obeah
the hobo
the birdman
the picker
the pecker
the unpopulated presence
the spinal vernacular
the blood-succored
the irrational epistemology
the perduration of certain jellyfish
the twelve animal forms of xing yi quan
the twelve bonang kettles of the venerable roaring sea
the moon-flat affect
the emblems of motion deployed in trees
the low areas water collect
the scapula
the plastron
the cowrie
the ash
the planchette
the haruspex
the bone dice
the boom boom ox
the foul church

the prison yard
the mansion on the hill
the several strong drinks
the dressed meats
the amelioration
the physic
the florida water
the kananga water
the 20 mule team borax
the fels-naptha
the absorene
the bartender's friend
the brillo
the durham's rock hard water putty
the murphy oil soap
the frank's kraut juice
the kirk's original coco castile
the medicated bismoline powder
the smith's rosebud salve
the allens sunshine diced rutabagas
the albatross outboard motor oil
the lawrence brand no. 7 ½ chilled lead shot
the champion spark plugs
the two-stroke
the take 3
the four-stroke
the five spot
the deep six
the straight mute
the cup mute

the harmon mute
the bucket
the plunger
the valve
the plagal cadence
the dizzy cadence
the bartók substitution
the bird changes
the ice cream changes
the backdoor progression
the sears-roebuck bridge
the aeolian mode
the locrian mode
the mixolydian mode
the turkish makams
the half-diminished
the head
the sus chord
the chicken grease chord
the block chord in
the dropped voicing
the bottleneck slide
the coricidin slide
the pocketknife slide
the premier amp w/
the perforated cone
the snare
the wall of tinsel the lights sparkle off of
the slapback echo
the verse

the trautonium
the croix sonore
the ondes martenot
the clarinet which enters slow & seems milling
the turnaround
the rest
the dramatischer alt &
the viola then, col legno tratto con glissando
the seikilos epitaph & the hurrian songs
the opening of the instrument
the opening of the ear
the reopening of the hippodrome
the closing of the commons
the basis of common law
the expulsion of the acadians
the introduction of counting
the reintroduction of wolves
the matter of britain
the discovery of zero
the labors of hercules
the inventions of archimedes
the solving of riddles
the feats of endurance
the transmission of pyrotechnic knowledge
the black cat lady crackers
the devil dog 16's
the black jack pirate 20's
the happy lightning
the nitrate lightning
the viper extra loud

the po sing peacocks (do not hold in hand after lighting
the kwan yick cock brand (made in macau
the three grains chlorate flash
the strontium salts
the cryolite
the incandescence of iron
the paris green packet
the mag star
the lift charge
the cheap heat
the double turn
the peek-a-boo
the philly shoulder
the coverup
the clinch
the false finish
the blanket finish
the odds
the two chiefs
the jacob's ladder
the cup & saucer
the witch's broom
the bronze john
the boneset
the bent nail
the dollar bill
the loose coins
the devil's claw
the candles
the rose gold

the rabbit's foot
the rail spike
the milk glass
the jezebel root
the golden corydalis
the rhodora
the dogbane
the cudweed
the pieplant
the bear's grape
the goat's rue
the adder's mouth
the white avens
the prickly ash
the mullein
the selfheal
the licorice
the lousewort
the lamia & the king
the knights of pythias
the veiled prophets of baghdad
the ancient mystic order of samaritans
the international order of twelve knights & daughters of tabor
the improved order of hepsatophs
the concatenated order of hoo-hoo
the leopard society
the false face society
the famous 14 demons of syncopation
the elks club
the cardiff giant

the mechanical turk
the feejee mermaid
the piltdown man
the theft of fish
the oath on the iron
the girl in the form of a wolf
the spirit in the blue light
the obstinate wife learns to obey
the hanging game
the blood-vomiting game of 1835 featuring
the secret inoue house move &
the three ghost moves of honinbo jowa
the campbell dirigicycle
the black assarca shipwreck
the halfremembered hulls scuttled in graveyards
the clovis culture
the mississippi mounds
the heavener runestone
the tunguska event
the french connection
the lexington cure
the manhattan project
the trinity test
the roswell incident
the memphis sound
the dow jones
the national average
the earned run average
the federal league
the players league

the continental league
the national association
the american association also known as
the old beer & whiskey league
the massachusetts game
the knickerbocker rules
the dead ball era
the baltimore chop
the cleveland shamrocks
the scranton miners
the fort worth cats
the tabasco plataneros
the santurce cangrejeros
the homestead grays
the pensacola dons
the spitter
the cutter
the yakker
the eephus
the legs the arms
the flannel bag of mixed ingredient
the bronze john come again
the eccrine gland
the apocrine gland
the age of heroic medicines & its reprobate doctors
the venesection
the toxic nostrums
the paregoric which is to say
the camphorated tincture of opium
the calomel which is to say

the horn quicksilver
the trivalent antimony which is to say
the tartar emetic which is to say
the mrs. moffat's shoo-fly powders for drunkenness
the ya hom five pagodas powder for alertness
the dr. pierce's golden medical discovery
the mclean's volcanic liniment
the hitch's cough cure
the hoyt's cologne
the hopkin's catarrh
the cubebs & copaiba
the true dalmatian insect powder
the atropine & serum
the lancet & the lye
the quinsy
the canker
the tissick
the gout
the abasia
the aphasia
the apoplexy
the ague
the grippe
the grocer's itch
the hysteria
the horrors
the addison's disease
the ragpicker's disease
the spanish disease
the parkinson's disease

the gambler's fallacy
the miller's word
the whore's bath
the ploughman's lunch
the physician's friend
the prisoner's dilemma
the knight's tale
the host
the mortise & rim
the barrel & curtain
the hasp & staple
the talon & the toe
the tumbler
the bump key
the berlin key
the hinge bolt
the hook bolt
the flush bolt
the follower
the cross rail
the racket
the reign
the wood duck
the warbler
the martin
the smew
the quetzal
the curlew
the mealy parrot
the whimbrel

the pelagic cormorant
the hooded visorbearer
the great tinamou
the laughing gull
the pine flycatcher
the blue-throated motmot
the bar-tailed trogon
the stygian owl
the cactus wren
the i'iwa
the toucan
the finch
the fine volume
the one that suffered
the crease
the smear
the stain
the soiled endpapers
the best fiction, written in
the secret inks
the secret inks is everything
t-roy was everything
dorene regular owned a newspaper
willie p. didn't own things
so malcolm didn't too
eddie's harmless
mama's preggers again
the taxidermist talked a streak
said the dendrites made him curse
timmy who the eff is filch

how many rick in a cord
who are your people
exactly where's your face at
your mountain apocopic mouth
ginger mae & her three daughters
wednesday done gave a shit
friday he don't care
jim the more he drinks the more he sees
menelaus he julep
heraclitus wept
king mithridates found frogs to eat
& filled his dish w/ butter
& taxed the moon
his vapors & ass
pedro hailed into little headed summer
the farmer wounded something
esmerelda could comprehend
be esmerelda
be the sea
be swept upright, swept outward
be god, christ
be divinity
be johnny milton
be the author's suspect memory
remember the wheaten bread
be noxious overmuch
be inviolate overmuch
be lamentable, be perfidious like time
be hoary & tipsy & crisp
be phrenology's extrapolations, meaning

be some mind hanging
repent something
prove a fact
get drinking that
look on now
look me once pretty
lock the damn house
talk to dorene
take the pain from her leg
church the heat mouse
horse out of suffering
have you some hound
name your firstborn
name her 'moody yawper'
go warm the coil now
go pucker up now
lay to your sovran
pick up that knife
now sumac
now ironweed
now trochaic substitution
now call upon a syllable
to enlimb a stark return
to transubstantiate, metempsychose
to feel
to be too clean a line
to inhabit
to unlimit
park it
lemme his jug

I am of the black mortal bane *kāla-rātri*
& to the city I come

NOTES

NOTES

Some language was appropriated from, or inspired by, other works.

Blake, William. Letter to Thomas Butts, 1802

Boulaese, Jean. *Le Thrésor et entière histoire de la triomphante victoire du corps de Dieu sur l'esprit maling Beelzebub, obtenuë à Laon l'an 1566*

Connor, Steven. *Dumbstruck: A Cultural History of Ventriloquism*

Deren, Maya. *Divine Horsemen: The Living Gods of Haiti*

Duncan, Robert. "A Song from the Structures of Rime Ringing as the Poet Paul Celan Sings," *Ground Work*

"False Lamkin," Child ballad 93 & in particular the version sung by Jane Robinson of Fayetteville, Ark., March 1957—Mary Celeste Parler Collection, Reel 350, Item 5

Jeremiah 6 : 1

Jones, Barbara. *Design for Death*

King, Ben E. "It's All Over," Atlantic 7" AT 4007

Little Richard. "Tutti Frutti," Specialty 7" XSP-561-45

Nightmare Alley, 1947 film, dir. Edmund Goulding

Pindar : Pythian II

Ramsey, David. "Prayers for Richard," *Oxford American,* Winter 2015

Sexteto Boloña, ‹‹Te Prohibido el Cabaret››, *La Historia de Son Cubano: Roots of Salsa Vol. 1*, Folklyric LP FL 9053

"Shady Grove," American trad.

Stephenson, Will. "A Killing in Pocahontas," *Arkansas Times,* Apr. 26, 2015

Strindberg, August. *Der Pelikan*

The phrase "bad sign of water moving upward" is from David B. Applegate.

Indeterminacy, or (conversely the pattern is a semiotic translation of *Meshes of the Afternoon,* dir. Maya Deren & Alexander Hammid, 1943.

In addition to the Will Stephenson story acknowledged in the preceding list, The white house by the black river incorporates a number of details from regional crime reports.

THE CABARET is for Tim & Whit & ________

Anyone wishing to contact me can do so by post—

C. Violet Eaton
P.O. Box 234
West Fork, AR 72774

YES   NO

A B C D E F G H I J K L M
N O P Q R S T U V W X Y Z

1 2 3 4 5 6 7 8 9 0

GOOD BYE

ABOUT THE AUTHOR

C. VIOLET EATON is a poet living in Arkansas. His first full-length collection, *Some Habits*, was the winner of the 2013 Omnidawn Open Poetry Prize, selected by Forrest Gander. *Quartet* is his second book.

AHSAHTA PRESS

NEW SERIES

AHSAHTA PRESS

SAWTOOTH POETRY PRIZE SERIES

This book is set in Apollo MT type with Futura Standard titles
by Ahsahta Press at Boise State University.
Cover design by Quemadura.
Book design by Janet Holmes.

AHSAHTA PRESS

2018

JANET HOLMES, DIRECTOR

MICHAEL GREEN

EMMA HELDEN

KATHRYN JENSEN

BRITTANY O'MEARA

TESSY WARD